IN SEARCH OF HIS EXCELLENCY

by

Anna Marie Kelly

RoseDog Books
PITTSBURGH, PENNSYLVANIA 15238

IN SEARCH OF HIS EXCELLENCY

CIVIL WAR PENDING

CIVIL WAR PENDING

SUMMER'S BOUQUET

Agony over?

    Is it?

    School's out.

    Summer safe.

So far, so good.

    Warm, hot, super-hot

Sun's out, sun's in

Beasts prolong their pleasure.

Occasional red flares.

Fires smolder.

Ambers of remembrance.

COUNTERFEITS

What are you going to do with it?

    I'll take it to the IRS.

    I'll burn it.

    I'll roll it up and smoke it.

    I'll save them all in a jar.

    I'll have madd money.

I want my $170.00 back - Secret Service!

Where's my matching funds???

CONVERSATION WITH MYSELF

"Heavy warnings"

   "Too much snow"

   "Way too cold"

      "Where's the heat?"

         "Boy, it's warm in here."

"Have to slow down."

"Change that schedule"

   "Where are you?"

"That tower seems down."

"Looks like more bad weather."

It's the rails you know."

   "Where are you going?"

      "They have a flat tire."

"I'm going to bed."

"Shut those lights off."

   "It's too dangerous."

      "I'll get up a little earlier."

"She talks too fast."

"It doesn't look good."

"What a crook."

"What'll we do?"

"mmm mashed potatoes and gravy."

"Sit tight!"

"Don't say a word."

"Don't answer that phone."

"What'll you say?"

"Have a great day!!"

THE LEGACY

Moving objects both

Large and small,

Clang, clang, goes the meat slicer

The cross on the wall

Solemnly sleeping til death

Knocks on the door.

Having fever and squalls

The paint chips to the floor.

After mass recital and flu,

He takes off for the

Cleveland Diocese, too.

Unprepared for rituals of Satan,

Having nowhere to hide,

The organist is impatient

Unprepared for holy communion

He carries on in staring form shaken.

He was ditched for the wrong pitch.

Now has Jesus on his side.

CANNIBAL RISING

They had cannibals.

The police said they could do nothing.

They stared at me.

They joined the confederates.

The cannibal army.

The Civil War again.

Cannibals against the North.

DEBT IS CONSUMING

I remember

Time as a busy working day

Hours six to six

Like people eating crabs

And sleeping, evening out,

Dinner at 10.

Now TV at 4 a.m., naps at 11. Raps

Raps on the door,

Batman asking for my resume

I think and dream of the dead roadkill

And another funeral.

MAN

Mechanical, machines

Nuts, bolts and screws.

Graven images

Inordinate affections,

Fallen, unfaithful,

Seeks effort, builder minds –

Mindless militant.

Drug oriented

Pleasure seekers. Whoa man,

Lays seeds, like weeds,

Cats and dogs - off to another,

    Instinctively.

Travel,

Crash,

Crash landings,

    Place to crash.

LIONS, TIGERS AND BEARS — WHERE'S THE HOT AIR BALLOON?

Michael, when we first met, reminded me of the lion on the Wizard of Oz. He had long wavy brown hair and was very muscular. Michael was a coward.

Rob, my ex, who always hung around, reminded me of the tin man, with no heart, calling me banana rator, Bator, my pet, daisy, cute and shy sometimes, with salt and pepper hair. He loved to have me cut his hair, very kind and soft but yet he had no heart.

Gary, Michael's and Rob's best friend, was skinny, funny and the tallest of the three, black hair. He once owned a cleaning business cleaning L and K Restaurants and Sea World in Aurora, Ohio. He went from $140,000 a year to cooking chicken at Racissi's Restaurant becoming addicted to drugs and alcohol. Gary is now in chemotherapy and is taken care of by his son. He had no brain. He reminded me of the scarecrow.

BILLS, BILLIONAIRES AND DOLLAR BILLS

Big bad Bill,

And his petit fleur.

He ate a lot of children,

But he wanted more.

DO YOU EAT MEAT?

Do their teeth rot out?

Do they wear dentures?

Do they eat their disease?

Are they insane?

Do they become cavemen?

Are they violent?

Do they start as addicts?

Do they dress up a lot at the Masonic Temple?

Are they pedophiles?

Why do some look dirty and others have money?

Can they digest their stomach and bleed?

HYSTERIA MOUNTING

The bills are waiting...

Still no freedom.

Held her to pay her dealer?

What is this all about?

Lots of crashes and skids—the rivers are melting

Something out of a movie. No one answers - Dorrance?

No life. Dead – phones are dead –

Left on hold.

Akron pipe bomb?

Vampire landlords?

The dead grandma and husband?

They left together 20 houses?

Closing costs –

Skids and skidding, drones over D.C.?

They made it back safely - What's up?

Got to send her money - hysterical.

I paid 45,000, where are your ears?

What planet are you from? Cops and robbers?

Send her the moslems,

Can she scam all those innocents?

Or maybe not so innocent - pipe bombs.

I hate war - send her money.

A DISTANT RUNNER

There isn't a time in history

I can remember with so

Few and far between.

The poisons fill our air

As nerve gas, sarin, agent orange

Shots to beautify the complexion,

Paralyze with dart frog

And fry them

Sterilize their minds

Making of stiff skeletons

With long gates.

Shots in the night,

We wander to our chosen

Duties,

As if the world is still

Twirling around.

Isis hits every corner of

Our universe and

Singing fills our pastimes

As wailings fill our streets of

Homeless children

Lost or dying.

Long faces we remember

Our hearts feel empty,

Our souls have left us, flittering

Out while we slumber.

There isn't a pillar,

Only cars with memories

Of human beings and

We avoid the new technology not to

Hear a distant cry

Or imagine a vain thing.

Our walls are stone blocks

Our apertures an

Arch of iron fences.

We walk to the stores as

The crystal meth has

Turned to dry mouths, memories

Distant, faces unrecognizable.

Our cravings are watered

Our waters are dirty.

Another day tomorrow, weather

Turning in constant derailments, HTML's search.

Keep moving til we find

The watering trough enough for

A multitude of runners, hoards

Of horses on wheels,

Chocolate, the love of lovers,

The gift of gab, honey, the waiting,

With hand open

Pathetic, he says in his harshness as

He wanders from one crop to another.

Breathing, seconds to ponder,

Hundreds gone,

Thousands missing,

Millions dead or await the forage.

Up and above we keep from the

Starving mouth

That yearns to converse brightly,

To our dismay, of course.

RAILROAD DETECTIVES

We're being railroaded

In the Civil War

Where transcontinental was born.

We're being railroaded

Where jeeps confiscate their groceries
    for their fat little bodies.

We're being railroaded

Where men can't find jobs,

But we need you forever.

We're being railroaded

Where the people watch as neighbors

Flee and are taken away

    In groups by men with badges.

GODLY SARCASM

Instead of sending

300 billion to Afghanistan,

We should raise minimum wage by 5 cents.

The news said gas could go up to $4 or $5.

We need hybrid bombers.

Instead of taking God out of everything,

Let's take dog out of everything.

We should start with hot dog and doggy, dog, dog.

DEAD IN OHIO

WWII

    Millions dead in days.

No cocaine at

    Golf tournament?

No heroin run

At golf tournament?

Opium gone?

Germany bankrupt?

No maceration pits?

No ships?

    Postal naval ships

in Charlotte, North Carolina

    from Germany?

Hospital invasions?

Like Syria, bombed after

    doctors shot for hiding morphine in caves.

6 dead yesterday,

    unexpectedly.

Laced heroin,

    680 dead in Ohio.

Awful tasting

    McDonald burgers?

LETHARGY

After dad died it was back to the psychologist,

Melancholy, lethargic, unhappy.

      Was all the schemes of events.

Drudgery pulling myself up to getting up.

No real game plan.

No real lifestyle or creative juices

      Or professionalism or career.

Working three jobs to pay the utilities.

Couple of bucks left over for all my month's work.

No monkey business. Weight gain depressed me more.

Where was dad, I wondered.

He went so suddenly,

I wanted to make a good impression on him.

Not a drug addict, drunkard or fool.

Show him progress but I made him sad.

He gave up.

My phone disconnected,

Not even hearing a few last words.

He could have lived longer. He could have been
    our link to civilization and lack of poverty.

I could have asked him if anyone in the family

Was a diabetic before he died.

There wasn't a lot of thinking time.

WE HAVE NO LEADER, NO STRONG RIGHT ARM

There is no leader to conquer this dilemma.

God only knows our destination and destiny.

Pee on indoctrination.

Will the flames engulf your riches and make you a poor man?

Will you come to know you are nothing more than a mortal peon like ourselves?

Will you ask for mercy?

You're in your imagination.

We ignore you, you're in your phenomena and virtual realities.

GRADUAL EXPIRATION DATE

Slowly he dropped from the heavens.

Wonderful, wonderful life,

Wife and children.

Slowly his health left

Flailing eyes and legs,

His job deteriorated,

Booze, cigarettes and girls

Were one of a past of hellacious activity.

Relatives passed on weakening his

Memory and his stability.

I CAN HEAR THE WAR

Civil history is

Front page headlines.

The marijuana, the hemp,

Cotton fields, northern

Clothing extremists,

Counterfeit 20's.

"I can't cash these in."

They avoid the people

With the yellow ink pens.

The banks can't accept them here.

And borderline south,

It scares me.

Money is short, the banks closed,

The stock market is sliding

Daily, twentieth day

in a row.

The northerner's don't

Know this.

The Ravenna arsenal

If full of machine guns.

Slave trade is plenty,

Especially at the NEC Golf

Tournament.

The games have the

Heaviest trade,

Soccer Federation,

Federation of the Blind,

World Federation of Wrestlers,

Even LLC.

ABORTION KILLS

I'm sorry to hear

Your mom has lime disease

And had to sell the

Farm to move to

Warmer climates.

She has always had

Complications ever

Since she had her

Abortion at 18.

I was 15 then but

The memories are

Very prevalent.

Both you and Jeffrey

Were difficult births

And she was on bed

Rest for both of you.

A WOUNDED, GREEDY BUSINESS

Wounded. I've been shot down

35 times now. They can't find me anywhere.

But I did get a bill from fifteen years ago from

Bank One.

Maybe they remember me.

But youth is swallowing up the jobs,

And some youths are in the traffic of drugs

And humans.

What do they want with this old biddy?

Do people look for crack money everywhere they turn?

I am not supposed to say this because

People get angry when I say this.

They are frightening. The thought of not

Being able just to order supplies or read a recipe

Or even start your own business without a mobster

Or a banker breathing down your throat.

I've decided not to try again.

If I make it through this heavy trial

I am not going to attempt anything outrageous.

They hold hostages. They need maybe $35,000 a week for heroin.

Again, the CEO corruption,

The pushers owning the children.

The Children Services from Hong Kong,

The nurses overseeing the psychiatrists again.

Let it all fall down.

Like John D. Rockefeller throwing his money off

The sky scraper.

Did he need all that money?

Did Martha Stewart need all her money or could

She have given Goodwill her beautiful comforters while

She was in jail to clothe the little children.

But what headlines of charity would have been hers.

The outrage of Brown, giving to the poor.

Giving to the destitute.

She had plenty of time to think while in West Virginia

But it was all about herself.

I feel I could get up and save a life and maybe if my background

Check passed, I could work in the hospital again.

But who is going to save me?

Today, want to be saved.

I want to have Jesus come into my life.

I'm not being facetious. He has had his presence be

Known to me. He has clothed me with garments

And his glorious radiance had shown down upon me but

I need it once again. The angel came to me and picked me up.

Maybe I'm late in thinking, maybe they are out there and coming
   on black

Horses. Maybe they're racing toward destruction.

Maybe I won't see the end. Maybe my end is near.

Maybe my end is here.

How do I get out of a rock and a hard place?

How do I put my finger on what to do?

Do we scream out for a ghandi to lead us out of repression

And captivity? Where is Gandhi and a black Muslim has never

Been my ruler or my leader. What do we do?

I rely on Christ. I have to hold on to that thin red line.

Maybe if I laugh hard enough at absurdity my mind won't

Think so hard.

Maybe a cup of coffee will end another optimum of anxiety.

They stole my identity. I am having an identity crisis.

I had an identity crisis as a young adult and

An anonymous religious man took me up.

Though I had to work and fill out a resume it was hard

To tear myself back and pleading that God would forgive me

And restore me. He was more than willing

But teared me like a pimp with harsh words and

I was to blame for all the agony I was suffering.

My heart went back to my lying dying husband where his

Ugliness was too much to behold at times and his woodpecker

Face made me wait to hear him snore in a deep restful sleep.

His rum and vodka bottles sat empty under the computer desk.

This was his second suicide attempt.

He had reached a bottomless pit.

I scrounged around at times with banks crashing, food lines long,

Houses empty, stray dogs, wild animals, desperate car commer-
cials.

People steal because everyone else does.

Identity theft to obtain work. Identity theft, computer destruction

To erase files. No one knows anyone.

I can't remember, there's no remedy for it is there.

We wouldn't want the billionaires having parties

We haven't found our way out of here.

We mellow out with a ray of hope.

The freezing weather distills us like alcohol

We're inebriated with the numbing of the pain.

Action is slow, I guess our unexpected blessing of leisure.

There's time to sort out the zaniness. Children seem to be

Missing from fraudulent caretakers.

Our souls ripped by vamps and vampires.

I come up for air, like a drowning victim in icy waters.

My soul repents of the sin notsomuch a crime to me

At the time.

A timely release when I felt was love yet flesh kept pulling me

Away from religion. I neither thought it right or wrong

Since others do it to find a mate or companion.

The law held me so tight as I couldn't breathe.

My child suffered, my children suffered, now I suffer.

Judge is still after Sarah, my lovely child.

He is ordering $1,000. A courtroom full of kids.

His habits higher than Donna Marie Flecks.

She was about $7,000 a day at the hospital.

But she went to drinking blood after adultery

After adultery. Heroin then blood, hemoglobin pills.

She doesn't want to go to the bathroom

Because of the mirrors. They don't show up in mirrors.

I carry garlic. Now Blade says to carry silver.

That's pretty heavy. But I always have a compact and a lighter.

They catch on fire and burn. Cheyenne has silver rings.

When she fired me her little face looked like a bat.

I told her the Mexicans have machine guns.

She won't get away you know.

Jim Moore tries to flee from Vegas

To the Ramada to Children's Hospital, now somewhere else.

The story I heard now is that Donna has let almost all

The cooks homeless.

I guess heroin can make anyone stupid enough to proselytize.

She was a sicko when she took over the department. Her mex

Friend and her Frank Sinatra looking fling. Bill Considine and

Old hot garter pants.

The world up there isn't husbands and wives. They are hookers,

Whores and adulterers and millions of dollars.

It's a place of lottery machines and spas and masseuses.

It's a 600 billion dollar a year industry.

He broke his back and ribs and nose and shoulder blade,

He broke his back, she broke her arm, wrist, her hip

And her pelvic bone, he got socked in the head,

He broke his ribs and he smashed his face.

She got shot 16 times, he got shot 18 times,

He got shot 6 times, he shot her and shot himself,

He drove off a cliff, he went through chemo,

He went through chemo, he went through liver transplant,

She went through chemo.

BAD NEWS CONSPIRACY
LETTER TO THE EDITOR

Don wants re-election.

I always say n.o.

Thirty years and lions, tiger and bears on the Copley farm. Don always said Copley was not his jurisdiction. So why all of a sudden the land dispute in Copley and Don will shut off their water if Infocision builds.

Don - the man that has hit men to coerce Rodrigues to sell Canal Park on State Street for a high rise building. Fortunately, when the 15-foot pane of glass was blown out by a rifleman perched on the Children's Hospital parking deck no one resident was killed in smoker's alley. A class action suit is in process.

Don - on the internet, fined $45,000 by the FBI for racketeering deals with the mafia owner of Minute men in Cleveland.

Don - with playmate pornographer Pamela Anderson of Baywatch.

Don - divorced from Mary. His own sister-in-law hates him. She works in a factory.

Don-cannibalism - I call him Lucy. Short for Lucifer.

Don-sex is his business, children, women and men.

Don - two heart by-passes, skin cancer surgery. He's starting to become a glutton for punishment.

Don - the man the city petitioned to limit mayor's office to two year terms because "Don is using drugs."

Don - Don is using drugs. Do we have to see this man get his head blown off by another drug dealer? Or maybe we can hear he's been stuffed in a trunk.

One big scenario. The drug people's struggle for their last hit of heroin.

Here's the clincher - Don's skull factor - Don uses human skulls to receive power from the dead (why the pasty skin), a voodoo culture he picked up from Joe White, old director of Children's Services. Does he keep skulls on his coffee table?

Question? Does Don's men pour acetone in Lake Rockwell?

Did Don kill the builders so he wouldn't have to pay the 4 billion dollars?

LETTER TO THE EDITOR

Don Plusquellic sees Pamela Anderson pornographer, in "Baywatch" series, actress.

Mary Plusquellic and Don divorce

Don is fined $45,000 by the FBI for his connections with mob owner of Minute Men Temporaries.

Don P is petitioned to be removed from office for drug abuse.

Don P swears at and fires parking lot attendant. Removed from office for two days.

Don P drunk and disorderly conduct outside Lux Bar downtown.

Mary P arrested on drunk charges, Mary P. dies in jail.

Akron city is in debt 4 billion dollars. Don P has 1500 lawsuits filed against him.

Aeros Stadium never paid for. Still owes $4 million.

Don P orders curfew for the city. Many pedestrians shot and killed by police if out after 6:00 p.m.

Don P fires Chief of Police.

Don P wants property at 50 State Street. Hires hit man to shoot out glass panel 15' called smokers alley from Children's Hospital parking deck.

Don P is taken in Class Action suit.

Don P fires 400 city employees.

Bill Cox, Summit County coroner is jailed three months and flees Akron to Trumbull County.

Tim Davis quits office 1998.

Don P takes 216 million in property taxes over 10 years.

Don P meets young woman in Columbus an aide, Melissa Barnhart.

Don P travels to Luxemburg, China, Japan, Italy for 10 years.

Don Presides in her home on West Exchange Street.

Carol Orosa gets mummy meth from pyramids for Don P and Drew Alexander, Sheriff.

Don P breaks up with Melissa. Melissa moves back to Columbus where she has a second home.

Don P has set of twins, in early photographs.

Don P's drug addiction grows.

Don P has skin cancer.

Don P fakes as Presidential candidate at John S. Knight Convention Center.

Don P collects $600,000 for his addiction in one evening with 60 factory owners.

Don P. tries to get Botox and stem cell to increase his stamina. Uses Children.

Don P. hosts dinner for regenecell at Quaker Square using 89-year old couple dancing the jitter-bug.

Don P. builds a stainless steel penthouse at Howard Street. Cost $700,000.

Don P. has 70 lions, tigers, and bears on Knox Road in Copley. Says it is not his jurisdiction.

Population of Akron declines 100,000 people.

Don P. doesn't let Infocision build in Copley.

Infocision builds on South Main Street in Old Bank One Building.

Don P and Mr. Howe have gross sex with Howe's secretary and kills her after she sees Howe pocket Child Support money.

Don P. tries to merge hospitals at Summa Health Systems to gain control of opiates, heroin, morphine, codeine and cocaine.

Don P. confiscates drugs for his use from street people camping out in wooded areas.

Don P. has 700 police escort his party of Nazis home after they get drunk at Mayor's Ball.

Dorothy Jackson, Assistant Deputy Mayor retires

Romanowski, Deputy Mayor retires.

Summerville, Deputy Mayor retires.

Drew Alexander, Sherriff retires.

John Soras, Director of Summit County Children's Services retires. Vernon and Barbara Sykes leave Akron.

Don P. ends annual fireworks display for 4th of July. Takes $100,000 from the city.

Don P. tries to build substation for Akron from Ohio Edison to control money for electric customers.

President Bush made him President of Mayors.

Don P. no longer President of Mayors.

Don P. tried to make the term of Mayor four years. Petitions were signed.

Don P. threatens Board of Elections officials that he must win or they die.

Brian Williams, State Representative fails against Don P.

Michael Callahan fails against Don P.

Michael Williams runs and fails against Don P.

Vera says friend from Cuyahoga Falls, Lisa goes underground with Black Book of clients for call girl ring at Children's Services under John Soras, Director.

Don P. and Sheriff Alexander are clients. He had plans to kill Lisa.

Giggle pants, Elaina

As of today

There is no peace in me.

Only emptyness for a

Beautiful little face

And a smirky little smile

Looking none the wiser.

Giggle pants

What a character.

I miss her so.

Each morning she

Would wake me up

For breakfast.

Her little fussing about –

Then standing at the

Playpen quietly

Waiting for me.

MINE UNRIGHTNESS HAST MADE ME SPOILED

The welfare trafficker, DMV the cause.

Rottenness is in me,

     Fear hast struck me on every side.

They clamor to speak

     But lead dumb to the slaughter.

Their winnings, their winnings,

And then no winnings.

Work it off, then prison, ignorant

Were we.

Innocent were they.

Mountaineers, mountain folk, kind and kindred,

A coal miner's daughter.

He cometh like Romanians, the vampire

Hearing horses in the present distance,

Cutting off privileges,

Some hide in the trash but the infant cries.

"When I kept silent, my bones wasted away."

HUMAN TRAFFICING

DRUGS, DRUGS, AND MORE DRUGS

TRAFFICING

WHAT IF NOT DEATH?

Shame, shameful

Living, afraid of

Prostitution, laughing

It off, madness, tempers,

Fear. Dropping off baby,

More fear, driver's license,

Job, tired, tired, tired.

Crooks, premeditated

Child abuse, babies sold,

Lots of loot.

Adoption agencies, stem cells,

Lithium memory for

Computers and cells phones,

Botox for wrinkles,

Fat old rich women,

Blood for vampires,

Life is strange,

My beautiful church, concerts,

Furs, symphonies,

Messiah, now closed;

A hobo sleeping under it's

Limbs with outstretched arms.

A SISSY

Ohio, Nevada, California chosen,

Lithium bombs made to escort

Them to various locations, No, I await

The end. My mountain is

Hidden in silence.

I shall not be moved.

He carried us through secret places

And adds to our belongings.

Children multiply and

Walls surround us like moats,

Boats launch and seafarers talk of

Capes and dishes of fishes.

I await this eternal bliss,

Like catfish in fresh water.

He speaks so vainly of his

Monstrosity like the Kosovo brain surgeon,

Or Nashville cats at Vanderbilt.

REGENECELL

All became addicts and joined Hitler.

They hailed him and forgot God.

Their need to survive became their eternal death.

They ate through Botox, stem cells, regenecell,

Cocaine, heroin became their source of denial.

They hated God and his likeness,

All became as dross, their bones wearied and their

Skin died as parchment in the sun.

MACY'S COACH BAG

No tears have poured forth.

A stiff neck, an empty heart.

Paralyzed in another insane act.

Natural disaster?

No. This is the eighth wreck.

What to do?

They want money. The bail, the impoundment.

Another $3,000 or $4,000 lost but who cares?

It was not your toil.

Why do you steal our minds away?

When work and profit move along and

We understand this?

Do you want us to help heal you of your pain?

Do you want us to drag him to justice?

Will it end there?

The electric chair,

The serial killer going down

Into history or we watch the building of war

And many dead and "who gives a hoot?"

They sell their children,

They walk away hopeless,

Though millions of churches stand

Open of every denomination,

Every day.

Can you walk away from sin

That feels so good and is so gratifying

For that moment?

Someone loves you, you seem to say.

ANOTHER DAY AWAITS
LIKE A GAME CALLER HUNTER

This day no progress.

Will I go to sleep tired from nothing.

From having to wait.

In the chamber of horrors.

I have no place to rest my head.

The screaming sirens add to the remedy.

Still clinging to an old fashionable, old fashion style,

Comfortable yet out dated.

Another door closes, another opens,

Maybe heaven's knocking on my back door.

COOL TALE OF TERROR

Dampened hair

So neat, so blonde

The German spewed another

From its larvae,

Snake eyes like

Steve Simmons and Reardon

Basking in the sun.

Soaking its glow from

Its childhood

Incest and cannibalism

Another snake spawned from

The factories of cocaine, heroin,

And opium, Germany, the

Naval Postal Fleet and our

U.S. Post Office.

LAYERS OF INFLUXUATION— LINE UPON LINE PRECEPT UPON PRECEPT

William Cox

Took his bribes for $150,000

To cover all the autopsies,

Haunted laboratory was 70 skeletons full.

I never want to go back. $700,000 home in Hudson, spent 3 months
time in the Oriana House

Took off for Trumball County.

Energy plant was closed

Caught on fire while we were out of town.

28 bodies were lined up

Found in the trash.

His chief of police finally

Was terminated after breaking his

Wife's arm.

Shot pedestrians on the street

Lots of pictures of Michael White,

Mayor of Cleveland at parties

On his wall. Drug parties, Drug parties.

My two daughter kidnapped by

Babysitter to lesbian girlfriend's house in

Portage Lakes. Both are addicts.

Monica Traveny CSB worker tries to drown

Them in her pool.

It starts to storm and Karen Barnes brings them

Back home. The girls tell me what they did.

I go to see Plusquellic but his aide says he has 1,000

Lawsuits per week and does not have time to see me.

I go to prosecutor's office, they send CSB to my

House to see me and want me on medication.

I show them a card of Romanowski, Deputy Mayor

And they leave and never come back.

17 years and 3 billion dollars in debt.

Michael Callahan doesn't win. No one runs against

Plusquellic in third term, and Brian Williams loses

To a crooked Board of Elections.

Tries to oversee Board of Elections and loses again.

They say State Representative doesn't have

Time to do both jobs.

Tim Davis, always has his stupid name

On the metro buses. He's so great.

The first one to go. He's caught and terminated

For taking money.

Where is integrity? Where is honesty?

Where are all the "good", or semi-good politicians?

Their sanity went with cocaine.

Meanwhile, back at the ranch, Lorenzo Pearce's

Ranch that is, lions, tigers and bears are getting
Hungry. Lorenzo famed cannibal, on disability
Often on television, has "farm" in Copley, totes his
Bengal tiger to Builder's Square in his carnival cage
His bear chained on the back of his little red pick-up
Truck, his lions in the humongous two story cage
Off Knox Road, with flood lights, small white cabins
And big wheel trucks run by longhaired, shaggy,
Toothless, men and women. Ghostly people at Builder's
Square. Lorenzo lives in a paintless shack surrounded
By mud. His son and grandson are killed by the lions,
But CSB doesn't get involve. He mythically goes to
Jail for a term but right back on the farm
With more lions, some 60, and reportedly, alligators.
One Beacon reporter interviewed him and said he feeds
Them live chickens.
    Chickenhawks are child pornographers.
The Children's Home open to the public the Haunted
Pumpkin fields in Copley. I never went there. Mickie
Witchy went and said they try to pull you off the wagons.

Joseph White, Director of Children's Services has law
Suits. One for 20 million for a three year old shot in
His crib in the head, and another for 14 million. The
Social Workers go on strike, all 200 of them.
Nothing changes. Joe White still there. 2003, the Children's
Home goes on strike for six months. The lions are removed
From Copley in August after the Summit County Health
Department files for health reasons and lack of vaccinations.

ANNA MARIE KELLY

Where the lions come from is not explained. The Beacon says the
Reserves would not take them and neither would the zoos.
Joe White is asked to step down. He refuses. The strike
Ends and the social workers go back to work December 29, 2003.
A new arbitrator is to be announced. Joe White is watched
Cautiously and on a continual basis. The Children's Home
Reportedly has 45 million in the bank. They received $18,000 per
    child when they are taken from the home. It all adds up.

I watched a PBS show on voodism the other night.
The voodoo priest stacks up sculls and bones of
Elephants, lizards, humans. They believe in the power
Of the dead. Voodism is a religion like Christianity.
Instead of fire and brimstone, they believe in zombies.
They poison their victims with a potion, do frenzied dancing,
Die and return from the dead as zombies.

Joe White reminds me of this along with his social workers
For the last twenty years.

I looked on voodoo.com. It looks like the sale of potions
Are popular in New Orleans.

Michael, my husband, is very sick now. He was on
Cocaine for years, running here and there for drugs.
In and out of jail. His dad, a mason, got him out of
Jail many times, showing his pinky ring with the swastika
To the chief of police. I think for some reason his family was
Raised on cocaine. Unfortunately, they have a lot of cancer

In the family. When I put my husband in jail

Twice, his Eastern Star sister would pay the police off

With a hundred dollars and he would be out the next day,

Even with a 450,000 bond on him. He became very

Dangerous, violent, always watching pornography and then

Gradually he became forgetful, tired, lost the use of his

Legs and now he has excruciating pain in his arm and

Shoulder and is bleeding from the rectum. I think it is sad

That his own mother and father would lead him to his life of hell.

I had a feeling that, Michael, being out of control, would

Eventually have his cocaine laced by his supplier.

I think that is what happened to him. I hope it wasn't the Zombie

Drug. The police said that, when I got sick on Pumpkin bread my

Daughter's boyfriend's mom gave me, that food has been laced

With rat poisoning, cyanide, crack, heroin, date rape, retinal

Crystal meth, acetone, cocaine (maybe even codeine). Life

Expectancy on cocaine is about 15 years. I didn't think my

Husband would live this long.

LEAVING GOD

He has hurt my heart over the years.

Pets, starvation, the poor, the impoverished,

    The elderly, the drunkard, the homeless,

    The orphan, little did he regard the widow.

The white robe made filthy.

EMPTY CAGES

Life is strange

My beautiful church,

Concerts, furs symphonies,

Messiahs — now closed.

A hobo sleeping under its limbs

With outstretched arms.

I FEEL HER LIFELESSNESS

I'm drenched in water,

    Soil, fresh breeze.

My soul aches,

    The pain of gases

      Passes.

Worn from worry.

Neck, feet, broken

    From so many

      Stabbings.

USE MONKEYS

Isis and Ice freeze us in our tracks,

Monkeys await, await their doom,

Our lights loom hanging fire,

While construction stalks us like ancient Dinosaurs.

We look for the crowds hiding in the mobs,

While few are chosen to be placed in an effigy.

CONSIDINE PUSHERS

Berghoff Street was

Plenty of souls,

Plenty of bread

And butter for the

Table of hardhearted men.

Slaves envisioned with

Glorious riches, tattered,

Torn, bought and sold.

Many devoured by

The lips of sensuality,

The souls governed by the

Law of moffits.

"We are not alone in this", is

Common knowledge among

Those patronizing sin,

Those piteously stolen from

Dear hearts always wanting.

Their pockets were full of rolls.

Their bodies were full of souls.

CASINO ROYALE

The good book says "royalty and

    All that good rot".

What a fat tale of

Gluttons and snails,

Csars and vomit and gromit,

Of pistols and snarls.

Roman's delight in

Seeing the flight of morans

And poor worthless carnage,

They bore their sluts,

Created from muts,

Their pink skinned fluts,

Their whoreish gluts.

They eat from the caves,

They rose up from the knaves,

They bartered, they sold,

They played hookey,

They grew old,

And made slaves.

RUSSO GLUTTONY

Russo Cartel

V.A. Clinic smells

Cars are overparked

Moved them in the dark.

Carts too small to tell

    Snow fell,

        Told a tale

            Tattletale.

Go to hell,

Russo cartel

We can smell

    Dr. Russo, you fairy

        Medical — too scary

            Monster's eyeballs

    Too hairy.

Hairy eyeballs,

    Too weary.

Patients disappeared

    Medical impaired

    Mandatory slue

    Feeling like glue,

Tall monsters

    Eat pizzas,

They don't shop,

    They hop

Ordering out

    Take their snout.

Rotting grass,

    Methane gas,

We dead and play dead

    Almost time to find Ted.

Rat-a-tat-tat

Names of mobsters

    Great commission

    Abomination.

ITALIANO SNOBS

Fat rolly polly,

Little pig tails,

Skin them alive

The others say.

We sit aghast,

Silence looms over

  The rooms,

Endless bliss,

Horrors of doom,

Where do you hide into the gloom?

Night stalkers,

  Night walkers

Night talkers,

  Night hawkers.

Breathless rogue

Enters the toad,

Red-eyed banchi,

Yelping dogs,

Starving mauls,

Endless hauls,

Bye, bye ya all.

Prisons stank,

Need to break

Piles of poo

Smells of doggy doo.

Hate fills their eyes,

Blinded by the rise,

Of Haiti and the great

Blah, blah, blah.

Fast mouth to release

To grant us peace,

That torches still exist

In the plantations (at risk)

A wrist, chains on their fists.

Chains on their feet,

Arms are discrete,

Filtering through the

Mountains dew,

Downhill, uphill, like Cumberland Trail

— Appalachian isn't frail,

Porn you dogs,

You unsophisticated hogs,

You speechless blobs

Of old-fashioned clogs,

We hate your style,

Your toothless smile,

Your ignorant comics,

Your beat-up chicks,

Your hicks.

You pick your nose

You smell like a rose—not,

You're snot.

You fart in your blue jean pants

You want to learn to dance,

You fraternize your fraternity

You worship your maternity.

AN ADDICTION PROBLEM

It refuses offers, gifts, laughter, joy.

The addict always cries out.

Yells. It hopes someone will ask them just

    The right question to set it free.

It is not fussy or ever funny.

It is not unusually clean.

It cannot work, it cannot groom.

It's full of self-pity and gloom.

It is too lofty to set itself at ease.

It cannot tell you a good story for it has

    no happy ending.

LISENCE PLATES

The "FAT CAT" in red Cadillac, pink Cadillac,

Did harbor the estranged

With properties to hold them captive.

Some without number, some without name.

Black jabba was king of the others,

That housed clothed and met with

The dealers to harbor.

For the rich and the toys of

all they would meet,

Murderers, slave owners,

Grand poopas, wizards, witches would eat.

Babies were wanted by

Their mothers in jail,

They were set up by the star

And their ingratiation was frail.

They are sent on their school day

And in August they wait

For the golfers' return

To the NEC Gate.

They excitedly wait

Not knowing what to expect,

For they have little ones and big ones

And a few men to delect.

For the millionaire's may

Want one or two,

Maybe a handful or a few,

Maybe a few men, even yet.

But the fat lady never wonders,

If they don't return, if they are

Cast by the wayside or the

Roadside to burn.

She knows there are plenty more out there

That need entertainment, too.

She knows that guns, they don't go

    To that trouble.

She'll open a meth lab if heroin

    Goes double.

Some marry their children,

Changing their names,

Some get doctor's approval

For more acetone.

Some go insane inside and out,

But happily gain from a sheriff or scout,

Foreclosures, second mortgages, apartments burn.

They don't pawn or gamble,

But look reasonably rich.

Their fanfare is hairdos, ribbons

Stare and a stitch.

Few speak from all the shock

From the coffee dispensed,

Since the day of their birth

To the year of sixpence.

The Fat Lady goes on while

The grandparents stumble,

As they ask God what is this?

Without a mere grumble.

CHILDREN'S HOSPITAL

They eat guts

Live on fluid

Drink blood

Make hemoglobin pills

Put heroin and other drugs

In the food.

They put cocaine in the food

Walk in and out of necropsy,

Infectious waste,

With plates

Have a moratorium

In the auditorium

For the children who died

From June to August

Hires a Mexican Executive

Chef from Las Vegas.

STUBBORNESS

Storms closing in.

Can't run to Mexico

Can't run to Puerto Rico.

Houston gone —-

Where are you going?

Giving up? Give up.

You're in another world

Another state of being.

He's shut out Florida - devastation.

Quantity erased.

Quality - hypothetical.

What's your world been?

Fun, fun, fun. Run, run, run.

Play it dumb, dumb, dumb,

You can only take so much.

 Now, feast, friends and family.

THE ICE CREAM MAN

Four broken

Arms in the

Projects

Now a white

Child, with

Three skinny

Siblings

The dealer

Threw one

Against the wall.

Summer with Ninja Turtles,

Batman and

Sponge Bob.

THE WELFARE SITTER

Names the same
Children with flaws
Hemming and hawing
Guffaw and guffaw.

Beastly fat surrounds them all
Sitting around her like
She's ten feet tall.

No one would guess with
The calm air she displays,
That all she wants to do
Is to play in a play.

She has them in dance,
On video in school,
Singing and laughing
Bidding adieu.

Her volume is rich
And her patriarch, too.
Court jesters would not be fitting,
For the part of her few.

Some are exhausted

Of the attention she craves,

Some are deathly sick

As ready for the grave.

With style and the cheeks

She gathers her chicks,

For welfare day cometh and

The grandparents still sticks

To it, and few know it.

Copulation, decapitation

All gather together

For their Christian relationships are

Abated as ever.

Rituals, rituals, witchcraft

And sorcery,

Bears on thrones in temple bare

Where hairy white men sit in their chair.

And poopah and hoopah

and stupah all sit

perched high in their underwear

not wearing a stitch.

their great leader, the Oz,

Is dining on abortery, adultery,

Adulterous spindly white hands,

Spreading their sorcery.

Lean over to grasp you and flip a bird

That will land in your boobie white soup,

With cascading spook and beheaded servers

Dressed in tuxedo suit.

They stand for an hour,

Disappear in the dusk

And dusty old chafers

Come out with a fuss

Over etiquette and

Ping-pong and tables of gold

And shoes without bangles

And whatever you choose.

THE OPPOSITION

Like two poles

    That don't connect,

        The darkness and light

            Moving in different directions.

Defensive and offensive

    Human trafficking,

        I am his evil, he is my evil,

            My pain, I am his pain.

DECAPITATED

There is a hole

    And a gap

Between the seen

    And the unseen.

This hole is

    Now being filled

With grief and pain.

I cannot overcome

    This pain

Though sorrow seeks

    To console me.

Laughter finds

    Its way

And silence and

    Solemnity.

I REMEMBER YOU

Ballet

    Tap dance

        Dance at Cuyahoga Falls Nan Klingers

        Became a dance student

          Became a dance instructor

          It was all wonderful.

You sang in the

    Christmas pageant

You became valedictorian

    And speaker of lifeskills.

        Fantastic.

You led a class

    And made a turkey

        Full of prayers of hundreds of

        Women in prison.

          Awesome.

You travelled

    You travelled to Istanbul

    You travelled to Greece.

    You travelled to Germany.

        Dauntless.

You survived

Plane crashes,

Hurricane Sandy. God was with you.

You kept in tune with the infinite.

You stayed school.

You bore two children.

Two lovely girls, just like you.

THE BLUE HOUSE

In the depth of the abyss,

I sit hands folded over my head,

Heart heavy laden with murders

And friends far from reach.

Nevermore have I seen

The painted faces of peasants

And the fever that dwelt and

Held them captive for so long.

Time evades me as

Few people venture in the closed

Open doors.

All I hate is gone

But the lonely faces still linger.

Shadows of faces remind me that I

Couldn't love enough and could not free

Their emptiness or hold

Them long enough.

How much love is strong enough

To conquer hate.

Anna Marie Kelly

Apparently they could not

Overcome the malice they

Held increasingly from one

Moment to the next.

JULIUS ALL GONE

Julius seems to have grown very evil over the years

I can tell he hurts Joanne. He seems to have joined the

Government in drug dealing, have gotten on cocaine, crack and heroin. He searches for sexual pleasures from afar even. I guess Connecticut must be an awful place to live now.

He became a total lust devil like Baal it seems. Adultery has driven him to drugs and now he is nothing and can't convince a soul that he is Almighty God.

Poor old man and looking for others than his wife, Joanne, "The Holy Spirit". What a weird ending to a wonderful concept.

DEAR JOHN LETTERS

DEAR JOHN LETTERS

BUTTERFLIES CHASE BUTTERCUPS

I hope you are well,

I think of you still

In times like these,

Enjoy freedom and breeze.

But alone, I think, that you

Make me well,

When my soul doest quiver

And swell a bright shiver,

The glow is warm, it rids the pain,

The anguish I feel, again and again.

Only now though, me thinks,

That you no longer think,

That I am that I am, a woman in pink.

The man that doest stalk,

Hast a whip and a hawk,

Looks into their eyes with

Fear and demise,

Who hast taken from thee,

The way that thou art,

And thou canst not find,

Opt to dream, to depart.

Be ready for he has

A part from the sea

A way to your heart,

By passage, deception, appearance

Or by tea.

So gather thy wits

And be smart

For if he takes away all

That thou hast,

He can break thy bones

And make a slave of thee still,

At last by lash,

Or by tracks or by splinter

And rail, or by ships, or by

Flying oblects or by sailboats

And sails.

Find hiding places

And dim thy lights in the night,

Neither should he know when thou comest,

When thou goest, be still.

Hear their voices,

Their snickers, their

Laughter, they devour the simplest,
The sweetest, the most
Delectable flower.

In schools they prey,
They, on their knees,
They pray.
In high places, in altars,
Back rooms, in vaults and
In high towers,
They stay.

I used to drive and
Park near your hive,
Where you'd be and
My hopes would arise that
You'd come to my beck and call
And say hello and goodbye.

However slight this may be,
Park nearby to the tree,
It may lighten thine heart
And give us a startle
That may arise in a departing
That is less disheartening.

The day may be lighter,

The sun may shine hotter,

The sweat of thy brow

May be more comforting later.

However, by night, not so safe

Wouldst thoust be

If the lion-man approached from

Behind of that tree,

And stoodst near thee and

Spoke in his grainey deep

Throat and wouldst see

That thou are not of the regular folk.

He may take thee and

Grind thee between his

Sharp jaws, and sharpen thy

Face with incredulous paws.

He may drag thee and take

Thee away till thou stank,

Don't call him by name

For he may just cower sweetly

And shrank and depart for he

Still has grown up and leaves

A place in our heart.

He comest, he goest,

Sometimes he is seen.

When the winds roar the loudest

We cannot hear the crunching of

Bones and the scream.

So be good and love God

For he watches us and protects us

And calls us by name.

His creatures he made,

The four winds,

God is the same.

THE END OF THE BEGINNING

Lion torment

And you rescued me.

Not fully,

    But set me partly free.

Bitter cold and

Feet unshod.

You rode me home

    With promises

    With soft answers

    And sweet, sweet, refrain.

Quietly interrupting

    My numbness,

        Took me in like sister,

        Brother, lover, friend.

        I called you.

You wanted more,

Anger upturning the

Earth from nowhere,

Where friends never

Lay next to me.

But drunken slobber

 And you understood

 In your solitary room,

Until shock took

You by surprise,

And like a mindless puppet

 Expressed yourself.

What grandeur of peace

 Surrounded my bed.

Somehow we're still

Friends and tomorrow perhaps

 The more.

But let's wait for

We cannot break away

And the drawing is far

More powerful than the parting.

PULLED UP BY MY BOOTSTRAPS

Six years now no one has come near me.

Maybe seven or eight.

I can be bold again.

I have not drunk heavy wine.

I find myself more powerful.

I have not fallen for deceit or the vain man.

Once more I can be alone.

Once more I can stand like a mighty fortress.

The vampires come and go in the night.

They are losing their viability.

FROZEN FROM YOUR SILENCE...DESPICABLE

Tried to care

Tried to cope

Tried to want

 Faint desire

 Urgent pain

No one there, again.

Hurt so deep

Can't sleep

Tried to pray

Time capsule

Remember me

Somewhere, oblivious express.

Empty caverns

Missing you

 Sometimes

You stop by

 My heart stops.

I watched you

Expectantly as you

Careen down the road

Picking up hitchhikers.

There you go again,

Remember me

You seem to say.

Nursing my pains

And the fresh face

That left a jungle

Of whimsical whores and

Incantations on my doorstep.

BORDERLINE DEEP CREVICE, LEAVING ME EMPTY

You've kept ample

    Distance and

    Fear has grabbed you.

God has a magic mystery

    Which I'm afraid results in

Metaphysical, para-psychological

Ways.

However, is it ever safe?

BOUND TOGETHER

Transparancy,

He watching us

The other world of eyes,

Becoming visible

Appearing, flying

To capture us, bring us up hither,

Jesus visible, golden yellow on mosaic cross,

Full of mystery, Jesus with blazen white, blue belted robes,

Trains of purple. Jesus, king of all kings,

Appearing to encourage, strengthen believers,

Song of songs. Watch as the tree bears many

Different limbs, watch as two blue jays drink together

From the fountain of youth

As the vultures sit above and gracefully fly away

Togethers, holding hands with giant wings,

Off to watch as the chipmunks, squirrels find each other.

UPON MEETING

I miss your closeness

    Today and yesterday.

Your feelings are unclear

    But your intoxicating

    Effect for weeks

    Has built up and

    Left me alone once

    Again with a hangover of

    Headaches, anger

    And despair.

I spoke too freely

    And my inhibitions

    Told a lot

    And my loss of

    Security left me

    Too uninhibited

    Now feeling uninhabited.

Today I left you

    Early and dearly.

LONGER WINTER

The cold of winter carries on

The cold of winter in a song.

The gold of winter we prolong.

As memories of old are gone.

The cold of winter, the bitter cold of growing old.

The cold of winter keeps you warm.

Keeps you on your toes or freeze your nose.

NASTY ATTITUDE

His

Don't call

Don't write

I don't want to see you

I feel sorry for

You're walking

I'll never go to church

I never liked you

I keep telling you this

But it doesn't sink in

You're in your little

Fantasy world.

HERODOTUS TWINS

Incestuous ones

Making the twins

And triplets

Chromosones split with

Herodotus overtones.

Awake, o'man, thou art

Peeved,

With studies so

Great to find thy source,

From within is the strain of ever

Remorse.

Typically the sin

The captives hate

Has of no one else

To relate.

For relations have

Formed one so rebate

That he would find himself

Reprobate.

Our founding fathers

Didst have one gain

That falling short of

That one name

Didst give another (the shame)

To reply,

That he was still

Greater still by and by.

That canst, though it

Seem the one too true,

For you and your own to bid adieu.

DEAR JOHN

I've had some rough times lately. I hope you and your dad are doing alright and that your home situation will remain the same.

I saw Casey and Sarah out front of the house in his car yesterday, sitting and smoking a crack pipe. They always seem high but I never could figure it out. Sarah took my car recently, last week and said she "hid" it. I don't understand them. I put $700.00 into it a month ago. I still have insurance on it, can't drive it. It passed e-check but needs tags. I was planning on giving it to them like I fixed the Lumina and gave it to Kathy.

This has become a real dilemma and I have stayed up all night worrying.

I cannot live in another situation like I did with Michael. I have to tell them to leave. Sarah is finished with one year of school but with her confusion she seems to be lacking in motivation and her plans to go to Spain in September seems impossible. Casey, a real mixed up kid is trying to destroy her with himself and all her plans.

One week he applied to five colleges, this week he is going to join the Marines.

THE FAÇADE

A project, a study

A learning process.

You have become a person of indulgence

In criminal behavior.

You are a product of two scheming rascals,

Playing with the fools for God.

They have become your entrapment,

Your success story, your power-

Hungry greed, your force.

You are not blessed though you have become

Blessed looking.

Your meth lab and gothic friends dwell inside

In dark cavernous eyes.

Your sweet smile and jovial laughter

A façade.

HEALING

You mellow out without the giggle and the smirk.

Your laughter lightens my heart.

I forget my burdens.

Your serenity makes me calm.

Your eyes brighten as you look at me and they smile.

It cheers my heart to hear your voice

I wait patiently for your answer.

Even when nothing makes sense, you make sense.

Your warmth, it covers me.

MEETING YOU

A soft pillow at night

I dream dreams of you

You remember my thoughts

A part of me, I eat, breathe

And sleep you.

I hope you leave a rose on my doorstep

I hate being careful

I'm being brave with love

Because I am empty and

A light begins to glow,

I mix stubbornness with fear.

ATTENTIVE

You are like the white Christmas

Sweet, festive, plentiful, full of joy and life.

You are fragrant like harmony

Synonymous housing and timber

You make me weak, like a muskrat church

Thrown over your shoulder in play.

You are a tenor and high soprano.

BEYOND THE WALL

Rob is gone

But appears to be strongly

In love with me still

And there is a channel he

Speaks at will

To me on where to go –

Like advice long ago.

Me thinks someone says

What is good for me and

Sometimes I say get

Behind me thee,

But Robert's soul still speaks

And makes me weak.

I sometimes wish he were here,

and I could call upon him

In time when there is no one near,

Because his heart and soul

Watched me where I go.

If I were 87 and Robert were here

And he 89, he would be my best friend.

When robbers murdered him with

His comical way of cops and robbers,

And who made the best scores

With Cowboys and Indians.

A family man, I wish you were here.

INSULT UPON INJURY

Finding identy

When there wasn't a

    Head on my shoulders

I looked here and there but

    I couldn't find where I was.

I searched for the before

    Within me.

Looking for the feelings,

    The surroundings,

    The words of kindness,

    Gentleness, and tenderness.

I searched for the people I blotted out.

That image of hatred

The face that lunged at me

    When I spoke.

Nothing would "register"

    "sink in",

Nothing around me

Was the same.

STUCK

Inside I feel grievous and pain

And somewhat fear and guilt.

But the verbal nonsense and redundancy and

Repetition makes me feel shallow and crazy and

So empty

FRESH AIR

Loosing you is like smelling a garden

Then going to work in the coal mines.

I don't know if I was dead or alive

And gasping for air, choking on my

Headache made me let all else go

And carry on with what was important

To me. My life, Not yours.

You forget quickly, what lust can do.

Your terror, I'm sure was enough to blame

Me for all the silence and emptiness.

CONFUSION, CONCEPTION, DECEPTION

Watched them come and go

Like the stars at night,

Daybreak saunter in like a cool moose,

Wading across a stream at night

A wretched owl overlooking the darkness

Its prey, the bats.

Looking congenial, but

Writhing, within, drunk to conceal

The pain.

Afraid of the light,

Yet desiring high healed leather, so cool,

So dauntless. Vulgarity, beseech me,

It seems to say.

I want that whip and lash.

SORROWFUL, FALLEN

John, you are my strong arm

You hold me up and lift me when I am fallen.

You tenderly touch me with your gaze.

You poke fun at me and

My laughter carries me throughout the day.

Sometimes troubles gather but you

Scatter them.

Little is beseeming to you.

I canst gather fruit.

My life is torn down as it is built.

Tomorrow is a morrow and

Another morrow and another morrow.

I see no hope nor long for it.

I scowl at the earth

And all that was made.

NOT SURE

Can we still be friends?

I'm going through some things.

Feeling things.

I'm sorry I said, "the washing machine broke."

You have your friends, I have mine.

You can't change 50 years of time.

You can't crucify all those I love,

Because you love me and want me for yourself.

I'll buy a cat.

There are different degrees of love.

Love me.

Love my cat.

We can't hide from each other,

Although there are things better left unsaid.

Can we be alone together rather than alone apart.

Sure, if guilt doesn't question what we do.

JOHNNY

I couldn't tell you how much you mean to me.

Because I have fear that if you would

Leave there would never be a dream.

Not even a glimpse of your smiling face and

My shyness applauds when you are near.

I can only say "hi", "how have you been?"

Because each time there is space

And you stay warm but whining I hear

And we still cannot be together

Because there is a block, a human block, I fear.

My insides say it screams out,

The meth labs say you're queer.

You prefer to let down to Nazis.

Nazis are too ugly, unimaginable.

We stay light and cheerful.

What do they know,

They are madness to cannibalism.

I can see below, they are gone.

Their air stinks.

BE YE PERFECT, FOR I AM PERFECT

Why is it that people so blandly say "Nothing is perfect."

Why don't they say life is "far from perfect." Or "life does not exist as it should" only Hitler's hate and murder spirit exist.

Love in theory can last, in fact, love can last longer than hatred. I think forgiveness is an excuse. The ones that sin expect forgiveness in the long run and has a fear of love.

If our laughter and speech keep us together, if the softness of the tone of your voice will always soothe my spirit and bring me back out of the pain and anguish of missing you and hearing the rattling of his scratchy voice all day, then we will always have to communicate.

Please help me with my pain. It is too deep to tell you on the phone.

It is too deep unless buried in your arms, to keep me warm, to always say you will be my friend and lover. You and I in the darkness never a soul to enter into our lives whatever brief, we are eternal, however, often, we are immortal.

We live, we breathe, we find each other again. The tearing away at the flesh, our spirits meet being crucified, our souls conjoin.

LOST

Finding identity

When there wasn't

A head on my shoulders.

I looked here and there

But I couldn't find

Where I was.

I searched for the before

Within me.

Looking for the feelings,

The surroundings,

The words of kindness,

Gentleness, and tenderness.

I searched for the people

I blotted out.

That image of hatred,

The face that lunged at me when I spoke.

Nothing would "register", "sink in", nothing

Around me was the same.

NECESSITY

They can't hear you.

Why?

They can't hear

    I'm alone

        Without you.

I'm hurt

    Will you tell me?

    Someday. I'll wait.

    It's my world.

        What's your word?

GREAT CELEBRATIONS

GREAT CELEBRATIONS, PROMISES

SERVER, COOK

Sometimes I wonder what I am living for,

To see 70,000 gowns and see them

Having all the fun, the mates, the dates,

The shining shimmies and shammies

And all the glory.

Where was my ballroom, my dancing partner

These years? I shook the hands of Presidents,

Football players, took home their roses left behind,

Took pictures with the producers,

Wore my silly grin, worn out shoes, and cockeyed bow tie.

AS NIGHT FALLS, DAY AWAKENS

Sleep, wonderful sleep.

Silently beckons me to a slumber so deep.

Silence and softness,

Holding me ever so tightly now.

Silence for hours putting time in a brown box,

Where the heavy log and day timer has ended.

I am a million, trillion things that are put to silence.

Awakening is like making another day work for you.

They run, they play.

Someday their day will be full of time schedules,

Deadlines, but mom is here, daddy will be home soon

And I have to see what's in the refrigerator

And play music and spy out into the tree house

As they march into the house and bring in more dirt.

CAMPING CANDLES

Made of tin can, newspaper, melted candle wax.

String and paint.

Burns approximately

One hour with no or little wind.

Inexpensive to create

Convenient to use,

And easily accessible,

Not cumbersome on camping trips.

Creates a flame about

Four inches in height and

Burns the area of diameter of the can.

A SMOKER'S TALE

Make the demon smoke, café latte, tappiocca pudding,

Give me a dollar for my smokes.

Put them in that pack ol'tabacci, Old tobacco road.

Smoke that smoke

Tote that smoke,

Brown stuff, black snuff,

Grizzly smell, moldy

Old toad, puff puff puff.

Half that stuff,

Old tobacco road

Find me a penny for

That smoke son,

Find me a penny

Tote that tote.

Roll that pack

Roll that cigarette

I need papers for my pack

My smoke is my snack,

Smelly chairs, smelly office cigars, cigars,

Get your cigars.

Fat guy, fat guy

Feed my belly for awhile

Run to the station for the smoke

Back and up

Up and back

Run to the station for my pack.

Flick a little ashes,

In my chair,

Flick a little ashes

In your hair,

Flick a little ashes

In my ear.

Flick a little in my brand new clean sink

Flick a little ashes, make the whole

House stink.

RARR'S HOME

Mr. Riffle owns 40 houses I guess; the numbers change occasionally. The blacks would strum up a conversation, sometimes, I really don't know what they are saying. When I first moved here he only owned nine houses. All the blue houses. He liked to paint them blue. I don't really believe that because the three next to me are yellow and white.

I assume he raised rarr from a baby. Where he was born, I don't know. I pictured him in a high chair, half man, half lion. Lion-man they call him. From the Book of Psalms. They don't talk about him but we see him often now. Rarr drove a small beige car at first, when I first moved here in 2007. I guess they taught him how to drive.

Mr. Riffle is the strangest man with his white pick-up truck and Riffle Properties on the drop of his truck. He always has crackheads or drug addicts in his houses, Riff-Raff.

My dad used to say Riff-Raff a lot when I was a child.

EASTER DAY

Easter is such a happy day,

With children going out to play,

The sun is out, the stars shine bright,

Jesus shines his holy light.

Over all the world he has

Come and gone,

Leaving us with

Heavenly song.

Come twilight we will look at the sky,

And we will try to reason why,

He came to save us, and

He answers bye and bye,

And succors us into a

Dreamlike state,

And hold us firmly forever

While we wait.

CHRISTMASTIME

I pine for thine

Lost in battle slain, pining

Pining in new found lost love.

Glorious evergreens exemplify the season

Of Christians and neighbors,

The glories of the colors of autumn have fallen

Apple and cherry blossoms finish the harvest,

The exultation of Christmas is due.

Flowers fade as winter passes its dearth

Upon the earth.

But naught the poinsettia.

Glorifications dim as the holidays' trim.

Outside is the tempest of war and darkness

While the light shines its brightest in devastation –

The celebration. Of newborn worth.

Heaven help us. Angels descend and fading earth

Is alive again.

We hasten to present to him a meaningful

Memory of the blessing formed from his incarceration,

The institution of deity readily incarnate, reincarnation.

Finding the simile of forms and faces,

Grieve not for he has us in our places.

Risen from dank, cold, dark death places.

We are tempted to stride in unfortunado

Into the unseemingly world of conditioning.

Our air is conditioned to treat us rightly,

While we press onward deteriorating nightly

From the unsightly.

While the bright lights of heaven descend glorious,

Its tendrils and minstrels victorious.

Using our gifts miraculous,

Our feet stomp cantankerous.

The pines' season is aright flowing, wreathing,

Holly, mistletoeing, and bright red and green,

Its holy day splendor,

Meaningful moments so tender,

As chops and chicken, duck and pheasant,

Dress our tables for feasts deliriously pleasant.

Our dream states, our nightmares, our visions burst forth

With angels' choruses dressed in furs and robes,

Stars in the pulpit, the praising voices melodious and

Harmonious.

Sprucing the canticles with scotch pine, spruce tree branches

Sitting back with glasses of scotch and wines to rest,

To wrestle with scotch tape, bows, gifts and presents.

An awesome wonder

As its sturdiness and strength carry on

With another year gone asunder.

Redemption from a cross

To a tree

Adorned with glitter and gold

To beautify thee.

As he hung his ornation

To redeem us.

Merry Christmas made Mary merry.

The crown upon his costly head

Woke him up while he was dead.

Upon the bed he laid

Awaiting the grave.

He was carried away to be staid.

Though he walked upon the water

He showed up late

And then was made great.

That was his fate.

Herod slays the firstborn sons

As sleigh bells ring hereafter

Wisdom brings frankincense and myrrh

Scents from the Douglass firs,

We forgive the slighting of God's children

To wit the sleigh bells.

The smell of the ether was strong enough

To blind a man of his tether

Then he was not ate

For whom those that didst hate,

The sight of his uncomeliness

And his uncombed plate.

Awaiting his resurrection made splendor.

SOME FLICKER OF LIGHT

I like that people are turning from their sinful ways.

I like that people are filling the congregations.

I like that people are being fed.

I like that there are more clothes.

I like that they are being delivered.

SONG OF JESUS

We walked you and I when thorns did crown my head.

We perished together with the waters that rose

And when we were dead,

We walked along the way and streams flooded our dreams.

We perished with the wealth to be and wed the one we gave.

Our hearts are swollen we polish our shoes

To be appropriate among the ones you choose.

The grave rises up, we can hear the mournful crying,

Canst understand why, but we keep a candle burning.

A tortured sound night sometimes day,

Someone held captive for our stay.

We did not walk away, we died in fear others

Would feel our plight, we rose early and didst

Our work by night.

Silently, silently we hearken to mournful bliss,

The stillness we could hear, the hunger of the mist.

DELIVER ME
HIS SAVING GRACE

You lift the fallen,

You have bound up the

Brokenhearted,

You release the captives,

You have delivered me

From the violent man.

Lord have mercy.

Christ have mercy.

You lifted those out of

The wilderness

You calmed the stormy seas

You divided the waters,

Those are your mercies

You healed the blind man

You raised the dead

You healed Job's wounds,

You restorest my soul.

ONYA

I am the Rainforest

I am vast

I am unemcumbered

There is no one here.

I am.

No one knows me

I am unblemished,

Unscathed

Unemcumbered.

My occupation is

Freedom

I am not disturbed

I am at peace.

I am the Rainforest.

    Peacemakers

WE BELIEVE
HAVE FAITH ABOVE

We believe in God the Father, He

Lifts us from all sin, he leads us

To safety, our journey he

Prepares The rest is known

By him alone By

Angels alone

Leading us

Home.

HOLY HALLOWED EVE

Halloween gratitude for harvest, food

Our genuine lust for the spirit, lust for life.

We are obliged to God for multitude of the living bread,

Words sown for our edification and sanctification.

The upheavel of nature turning our loaves into wine,

The bitterness of winter cometh. The sweet breath of autumn,

The turning our beds into hearths.

We unlike all creatures build fireplaces of remembrance.

Our charcoal is turned into crayons and our wooden logs into toys.

Heaven heep us this season as we scurry to bring in the sheaves,

As we ward off death with thanksgiving and celebration.

CLIMBING

Back home I want to go, back home.

To mansion with many rooms, library doors, land,

Finished staircase, the book room and walk-in closets.

Back home, a dream, not thirteen rooms but nine,

    Dad left behind open doors, portals of time, sending back

Memories of love he left before he left.

    I look behind and forward at the same time, going home.

A mansion in the sky Jesus prepared for us. He loved us many times

Spoke to us many times, chastened and hastened away our fears.

    I forget the jasper stones, the twelve fruits, the white animals.

I keep on a pedestal the Katherine cross and am reminded again.

    The Last Supper table with goblets and wine and Jesus and Mary.

Someday I am bitter fruit of Marah, bitter waters, the smell of thistle,

Seeking more life, finding coldness and the warmth of the fireside.

Dream on, another day of motion. Tears of defeat in the waking hours and tiny moments of change - maybe.

A purple Packard—my dad drove home from Japan. Driving on the waters I seemed to say, knowing neither where or when or how.

One for sale - the busdriver blurts out "a 1950 or '49, he says, "I'll have to see this."

Still climbing back home to Rockefeller Center Square and Chase Bank, David's bank.

Finding remnant's of time on e-bay, x-box, micro mini cell phone, internet, i-pods.

Where will old fashions be when purple haze, and passion fruit liquors are fad and "my ways are not your ways".

More furriers, the bitter cold weather warnings, still climbing, good money, not foreign coins the bus meter won't accept or the confederate 20's the banks won't take, lose twenties to the pop machines and secret service but never get a refund for your lost hard work.

Good money, the banker's cashier's check. Not married again to hide what I did with the last name or had the cards that will never be paid back.

Waiting for the nerd that won't pay me because I'm rich enough, to kick

Off with an overdose of heroin or morphine or oxycotin.

WORD PROCESS

Researches first, middle and last name of individuals.

Books are accessible through antique book stores,

Campuses and regular outlets.

Books needed are books on names.

Cornish dictionary

Baby name books,

Dictionaries of foreign languages,

Encyclopedias

Musical, brittanica, Bible and concordance.

The name store would research the names of people and places

Them alphabetically on a computer, word process the individual.

BOARD ROOMS

I am bored

 Board rooms are boring

 But alas, I have a

  VCR

 That I know not

  Of

And a car

Thank you board rooms

You are not boring.

THE DEED

Still, the shingles need mending,

The plumbing bill spending,

The rafters are tattered

Grass needs mowed in the spring

With all the hope that love brings.

Still, the house seems well,

A place to dwell,

It is a roof over my head.

Money well spent,

It went towards the rent,

And now I'm almost out of debt.

But a little bit of this and

A little bit of that,

Pennies in my jar.

It takes care of itself

A beat up old car.

Friends from the street,

Keeping things neat,

Rutabagas spring wild,

A great side dish

Blankets from the Haven

Slow mist from the lake

Keeps me cool.

Heaters from yard sales

Replacing rusty old nails.

Paint from some torn down garage,

Roof caved in

A lot of drywall within.

I seem to be fitting in.

I FIRST SAW RARR

There were several incidents where Rarr would be talking to men in Pick-up trucks.

He was younger then. He stood on the balcony of the white crack house, the two story manor.

It was probably colonial in those days but dirty now and always surrounded by pit-bulls, wrapped up dirty diapers and lots of dog manure. It was filthy to say the least. The trash bins and cans were always full. When I saw him climb the balcony, he wore a pink jacket. His head was hairy. He wore slacks. He had paws. The young black man didn't seem to fear Rarr. He playfully shoved and pushed his negro girlfriend along to the end of the balcony. Rarr was climbing the steps. The girl's face froze as she stared at Rarr. The young man took a step back and Rarr pushed the girl through the open door to the apartment and closed the door. What smelled like burnt toast billowed into the air for a few days

HOLY GHOST

Life has a long twisting road that leads to finding truths. Truths about liars, truths about suspicions, hidden truths of family members, truths of immorality, the truths that answer so many questions as to why.

The truths to crime, sin, revenge, anger, murder, assault. The truths to drug addiction, love of drugs, weaknesses, shyness, confusion, religion, temptation, hatred, self-hatred, abuse, self-abuse.

The truths about sex and about love. The truths of seduction, and disobedience.

Immorality or sin is constant. So is forgiveness, grace, repentance, and mercy.

But again, there is a sin which is unforgiveable. The sin against the Holy Ghost. The sin against Jesus Christ is forgivable.

This country deals in sin. The greatest sin is defiling the holy temple of God. Drugs and drug use deliberately sins against the Holy Ghost. This is unforgiveable.

The dealer acts as a catalyst between the man and the Holy Ghost. Man hates the Holy Ghost. Man tries to crack that thing that breaks away his flesh.

The dealer poisons him with heroin, cocaine, opium, anything that will take away that holy feeling called love from him.

The dealer become his friend, his private parts of his being, his secret society from faithful wife, loving children. The dealer promises him sex, sexual activity, sexual partnership, sexual gratification. His life is attractive, wealthy and invincible

Man knows his ultimate ending, death for dealing with the dealer. He knows his time will run out, his money will run out and he will succumb to the sexual advances and sexual act with the dealer. The dealer has been his close friend, his confidant, his liaison in his war against holiness.

He knows that his ultimate act will be his final act, the dealer will finish him off and his fantasy of blood, hatred, pain guts will be his ultimate sexual satisfaction. Another victory for the dealer.

And man will finally rest. His will be done.

The dealer does not approach the godly. He does not see the godly. The godly man turns his head in another direction.

The godly man sees and hears the sin around him. He hears the threats, but greater is He than he that is in the world.

GREEN SLIME

There's a monster in my closet

He's big and mean.

I'm not sure what color he is,

But I think he's fierce and slimy and full of

     Robust green.

Stay away from your closet,

You must, you must.

He'll gnaw on your shoes and

Cover them with slime,

Beware of his fingernails,

They're embedded with grime.

A continuous slime runs

Down his face

Slime everywhere,

From place to place.

His eyes are collapsed

Between his nose,

His grim smile stretches,

With each meal it grows.

His teeth are permanent,

Eternal, everlasting, forever.

He vaguely brushes,

Now that's not so clever.

But I'm not really scared,

Nope, not anymore.

I opened the door,

Just a toy on the floor.

But by any chance you

Meet this guy,

My advice is protect yourself,

Run and hide.

Katrina

GLOBAL WARMING

As death seems to be catching us

We watch as nuclear predominates the pages.

As Carl Sagan wrote years gone by

His words are "Thoroughly Modern Millie", catching

Up to us. Six hundred mile radius' resonate

And old plans of terror, escape, melting ice caps,

His glacial movements, not those of notes unheard

Of, but the cold frozen ice filling the Northern Hemisphere,

Whether soon or suddenly, enjoy it's re-creation, it's Ending so many
passages in lifetime.

The beast of "too much population" cries out, more war, More war,

more death, more death. But, God says, don't worry,

Beast, I'm making this all possible, perhaps it's a little bit too Much, for
even you.

The grim darkness prevails, the Brides form the resistance and

The Grooms add to the coming of the Son of Man. Taking the

Hands and binding them, they push to end the stubbornness,

Loneliness, the wandering, the searching. The Royals, Pippin

Middleton, and Emporer Hirohito's Granddaughter Princess Mako, the
long trains, blazing white, long awaited Paris Hilton, our royal,

Another announcement, another announcement, Jesus' brides, he holds
captivity captive.

THRILLS AND CHILLS

Celtics and Druids

Painting their faces,

Scaring us with masks

Around fire places.

Autumn leaves falling,

Winter is calling,

Freezing rains

Fill window panes

Frost and dew,

Storm warnings, too.

Prepare us for winter,

O, Lord hear our plea,

Praying for safe keeping,

Frightening dark paths

While children are sleeping.

Chills and thrills

Barbarians and berserkers,

Ghosts, vampires, freaks,

Turks and hunchback lurkers.

Milky Ways, Snickers, Ha! Ha!

Fill our bags,

Peanut Butter Cups,

Tootsie Rolls, Butterfingers,

That old witch at the door

That old hag.

Washtubs with apples,

Slamming car doors,

Hordes of monsters

Run to and fro,

Stepping on fingers,

Stepping on toes.

When our tummies are full,

We seek a deep sleep,

Away from the monsters

Away from the creep.

USE MONKEYS TO CONTINUE

Isis and Ice freeze us in our track,

Monkeys await, await their doom.

Our lights loom hanging fire,

While construction stalks us like ancient

Dinosaurs.

We look for the crowds hiding in mobs,

While few are chosen to be placed in an effigy.

Why don't you move? Like she's the towering inferno

Laughing her guts out, as she plays with inheritance like

It will last her kind forever.

Ohio, Nevada, California chosen, lithium bombs made to

Escort them to various locations.

No, I await the end. My mountain is hidden in silence,

I shall not be moved.

He carried us trodden through secret places and adds to

Our belongings. Children multiply and walls surround us like

Moats, boats launched and seafarers

Talk of capes and dishes of fishes.

I await this eternal bliss, like catfish in fresh water.

He speaks so vainly of his monstrosity like the Kosovo

Brain surgeon, or Nashville cats at Vanderbilt.

CHURCH BELLS ARE RINGING, SALVATION ARMY BELLRINGER

We haven't had this type of cease fire,

Where we wish each other Happy Holidays and

Cordial greetings, Whispers of death on occasion passes by

In deep breath

Whispers of winter whispy white hair

Casual attire,

Cease fire.

At arms length we

Stand behind counters,

Gradually the yearly custom closes,

Wondering if we

Can keep each other warm further more.

The phone calls quieted.

Red kettles, aprons, bells,

Singing, giving daintily sometimes,

But graciously accepted.

The warm bed awaits

After the ears are frozen, the singing

Stops. Christmastime

Tomorrow will end another year.

My heart drops as I ponder the

Boringness of a few empty days

With nothing ahead.

Pick 4 all over, every day, in and out,

The faces look fuller, brighter, smiles broaden faces.

It's here, it's almost that time,

The rushing of the rushes,

The red flushed faces.

New to me. Living on a gamble.

Winners, I suppose.

Lots of poinsettas left.

Wonder where they will be on

Christmas eve.

Do I have time to buy

One more beautiful thing

Before this spirit-filled God passes us by

And the stores close early again

And the lights will be turned off,

One by one the houses will cease

Their filling of peace,

Pulling in strings and strands of color

Until we wait for that moment of hoopla

Where we will watch the ball come

Down to shuffle in another year.

Cold January winds and blustering freezing

Plunging temperatures.

They are out there tonight

Some scrambling for a deal,

Some for 70% off, while others

Scrape the tires around bends

To send off another

Roll of pot or white powder

Laced for death or a fetal high.

We will know some in the a.m.

How the survivors swung on New Year's Eve.

A quick $10,000 for Bertonini's Construction

As they tear down another

Home for quick cash for the Mex-Tex dealer.

SLEEP, BLESSED SLEEP

My life is torn down as it is built.

Tomorrow is a morrow, and another morrow and another morrow.

I see no hope now long for it.

I scowl at the earth and all that was made.

I can't become a part of it.

I bury my head at night and dread the daylight.

My sleep finds a way in the darkness.

TOUGH LOVE

Christmas is here.

Black Friday.

Salvation Army Bell ringers

Christmas stores full.

Stress, fear, lack of money,

The children to feed.

Churches, Christmas parties, Christmas meals,

Toys-for-tots, free gifts.

Humans are a social animal,

Gathering together information,

Moving on.

The troops are home.

And so is cold weather,

Hurrying to get back to

Those extra blankets, snow shovels,

To work with.

Winter crisis, extra food,

Extra thick socks and hopes

Mom and dad, grandma and grandpa,

Uncle and auntie will

Supply me with warm socks

And underwear.

God feeds the birds of the trees and

They neither turn nor toil.

THE BRIDEGOOM COMETH

God has a direction for me

His arrows pierce my heart

Like a cupid.

He pierces my ears

Like a wedding day.

Heaven holds its doors open.

He glows bright,

He warmly awaits like ecstasy and

His eye close as in death.

Happy are those that seek His face.

For the bridegroom cometh and

Calleth nigh for thee.

Prancing through the driven snow

Like ice capades, She

Is adorned as in a closet.

AKRON U CALCULUS

I feel dreary, there aren't enough feelings

to capture words. Maybe the pressure

Is in the mind trying to remember

The next formula on the test,

Or if you've brought enough

Pencils to finish it

Yourself, is your cell phone

Turned off, or did you have

Enough pages in the thesis, she wanted ten,

I guess. I sweated through

MyMathLab, all news to me.

I went back and changed the password twice.

I'm not Walt Whitman sitting in his cabin listening

To the spirit filled air and the words of Animals.

This traffic, cars, noises on the streets, the irritants

Of human consumption

Is like an earache, you have to numb it.

ANNA MARIE KELLY

SCRAPYARD

Toothless mongrel!!

"I hope you're not

    Talking about my dog!!!!"

"Nice dog."

"What's his name?"

    "Scraps."

"Scraps??" "Hah!"

    "That's fit to

       Kill."

MANNA FROM HEAVEN

What is it?

The ongoing question

Time immemorial

Our grudges dismissed

Like a fruitcake arriving

From the farmer next door.

She combs his hair with her fingers

To hide his bald spot.

But wait.

What is it?

They disappear in life memorial.

Never cropping up until

We look for trouble.

It's the Belair or the Corvair.

It's the isms in our life. Catachism, stoicism, heroism,

Patriotism, baptism.

The turnip field we didn't notice

Growing inconspicuously until Christmas arrived,

And we had extra portions.

What is it?

Manna from heaven.

ROSES FOR HIS THORNY CROWN

I'm resting, for the foe is nesting.

Finally, his deadbeat dad, crazy young lad,

Animal history, drowned in his pants

Hanging from his dance.

Frightful theme, hear the scream

As his headlights beam,

Dead at last, nights' full blast,

Starlight gleams, heavens beam,

Bad news flunks, all the drunks,

Nights of splendor

For lovers' tender,

Can't fight the roses,

The Moses and the boisterous noises.

TRAIN ROBBERIES

TRAIN ROBBERIES

I Lose My Train of Thought

I think of solar systems and the cosmos and of atoms and quarks.

I ponder and wonder but lose my train of thought.

But as the dogs down the street begin to bark and bark

I lose my train of thought.

In church on Sunday listening to the pastor, minister

Talking about the devil and says he is sinister

And talking of things on high, to women in the pew, baby

Begins to cry and

I lose my train of thought.

The train of thought is chugging down

The line (the tracks)

It will be coming through your mind

As well as mine. Its fuel is freedom of

Expression, not repression, like political

Correctness, which will eventually wreck and wreck us

And lose our train of thought.

Brothers and sisters, our ancestors came

From the land between the Black and Caspian Seas

With Caucasus mountains to the south

Do not lose your train of thought.

Be silent no longer and open your mouths

Speak against the aggressors who want

To take over your house and want

To take your train of thought.

Okey Michael Kelly

Behavioral path

Black women on the hunt

No spears in hand

A purse full of food stamps

Isn't that grand.

Up and down the aisles

With their carts they glide

Get out of the way

If you're not on their side.

Collard greens and ribs

Sweet potatoes and more

Get out of the way, boy

They own the store.

Spaghetti and meatballs

The Italian way

They could not be satisfied till

They moved God out of the way.

Okey Michael Kelly

METAMORPHESIS

A meaningless poem

Wandering without reason

Through nondescript landscape

On roads without seasons.

Colorless leaves

On non-existent trees,

No fluttering of butterflies

No droning of bees.

There is no plot,

No heroine, no hero

Here one plus one

Adds up to zero.

There is no reason

Yet there is rhyme

But if there was a clock

They would be out of time.

No singing of birds

No breeze through the trees

There's no milk from the cows

Therefore, not any cheese.

ANNA MARIE KELLY

Here no dogs are barking

Not cats meowing

There's no wolves either,

So there is no howling.

No joy in writer

No joy in reader

No surprise in the writer

No surprise in the reader.

Jack London said you can't

Wait for inspiration

You have to go after it with

A club. "perspiration"

Okey Michael Kelly

BEAUTIFUL MUSIC
by sarah kelly

Thank you for the beautiful music in my life,

The whistling of the kettle in the early morning chill.

The soft whispers of the lilies as they sway in the field.

The energetic robins chirp outside on the window sill.

The cooing from my precious baby girl.

RAT CAT

Rat Cat was happy sleeping under the porch. As he awoken, there was a giant speckled toad next to his head. As it croaked softly, Rat Cat decided that he did not want to disturb its rest.

After the heavy rainstorm, giant toads habitually venture to protect themselves for fear of losing their voices. The toad began to sway and quietly moaned. Rat Cat arose and looked sadly upon his new acquaintance; asked the toad his reason for his silence. The toad said "There is no silence when I have spoken." There was a giant clattering of the sound of thunder intermingled with the whistling of falling trees.

Suddenly there was a giant cloud formation over Rat Cat head.

There were bones, chickens, chili, cat food, tuna. That Fat Rat Cat ate all that.

A MANIAC'S DESIGN

12 million in one night OVI test for alcohol and drugs

Best night out New Year's Eve

Bars, clubs, having a beer at the Convention Center

400 cops, the regulars, paying judges

Drug addictions for a year.

Best night out New Year's Eve.

Their quota - one arrest,

400 times $30,000 or more

Will make $12,000,000.

Best night out New Year's Eve.

They send out the drugs,

They catch the dealer,

Or the prettiest chick for their

Porn lab, their strip show,

Best night out New Year's Eve.

Their strip clubs, drug her,

Rape her, keep her a hostage,

Give birth for the Harem.

Old boy with Dallas. Say "Dallas"

At church, there's a hush around the room.

Guess they were on the same page.

Parking tickets on all cars on

High street - jail time, all premeditated,

Best night out New Year's Eve.

The Harem of one police

Officer, judge or sheriff?

With 9 wives from the prison

All tattoo ladies, one man (judge?)

With a hotel style home on Turkeyfoot Lake.

9 tattooed women on towels, 40? Children,

5 boys following him into the water?

One he yells at "Dallas", "Dallas",

"Dallas"? not behaving?

Talks to me? Take off your towel?

What a killer, what a murderer,

rapist of the Summit County Jail?

Looks like McCarty-Allison wouldn't

Go for that. Dallas - Uncle Dallas.

$30,000 a year - still getting $30,000 a

Year each? What a plan - unbelievable,

Going into cells – raping these women. Pregnant in

Nine months, until delivery?

Drug addicted women - would stay in a Harem?

No families? Men in military? Raped wives?

What happened to Sheriff Kennedy? Other

Sherriff beaten face? Crippled neck?

BLESS THE EARTH, O MY SOUL

Bless the flowers with rain
Bless the blossoms with hail
Bless the oceans as it harkens,
Bless the waves with the wind.

Bless the grass as it grows
Bless the grain as life sows,
Bless the magnitude
    When world awakens,
Bless the constant heart
    that is aching.

Bless the trees
    with tiny leaves
Bless O' springtime
    Sun, Rain, Mist and breeze
Bless the winter as it leaves.
Bless the agony as it grieves.

Bless the mother with
    Child, Bless the child with mother,
Bless the son, father sister
    and brother.
Bless all the families
    that unite,

Bless the red, white and
    blue, the good fight.

Bless the dung that fertilizes
    Bless the death that
        heaven rises
Bless our thoughts that
    are asunder.
Bless the dying breath
    of thunder

Bless the lightning
    That brightens the skies,
Bless our outer space
    And bries
Bless our place on
    earth that meets
    together
Bless the pathways of
    our feet forever

Bless our hope, peace
    and wonder,
Lord, Bless O God
    of Heaven,
Bless us with strength
    and warriors with heaven.